EDGE
BOOKS™

ALL
ABOUT
DOGS

JACK RUSSELL
TERRIERS

by Tammy Gagne

Consultant: Jennifer Zablotny, DVM
Member, American Veterinary
Medical Association

Capstone
press®

Mankato, Minnesota

Edge Books are published by Capstone Press,
151 Good Counsel Drive, P.O. Box 669, Mankato, Minnesota 56002.
www.capstonepress.com

Library of Congress Cataloging-in-Publication Data
    Jack Russell terriers / by Tammy Gagne.
    p. cm. — (Edge books. All about dogs)
    Includes bibliographical references and index.
    Summary: "Describes the history, physical features, temperament, and care
of the Jack Russell terrier breed" — Provided by publisher.
    ISBN-13: 978-1-4296-2302-5 (hardcover)
    ISBN-10: 1-4296-2302-0 (hardcover)
    1. Jack Russell terrier — Juvenile literature. I. Title.
SF429.J27G34 2009
636.755 — dc22   2008028889

Editorial Credits
Erika Shores, editor; Veronica Bianchini, designer; Marcie Spence,
    photo researcher; Marcy Morin, photo shoot scheduler

Photo Credits: All photos by Capstone Press/Karon Dubke except:
Alamy/Jeremy Pardoe, 12; Peter Titmuss, 16
Capstone Press/TJ Thoraldson Digital Photography, 6, 7 (all)
Getty Images Inc./Bruno Vincent, 9; GK Hart/Vikki Hart, 24–25; Tim Platt, 18
iStockphoto/David Chadwick, 17; David Safanda, 23;
    Frederic De Bailliencourt, 22
Mary Evans Picture Library, 11
Ron Kimball Stock/Close Encounters of the Furry Kind, 5; Ron Kimball, 15

1 2 3 4 5 6 14 13 12 11 10 09

Table of Contents

CHAPTER 1

A HIGH-ENERGY DOG

Jack Russell terriers are bursting with energy. These little dogs chase anything that moves. People seeking an active pet with a big personality don't have to look any further than the Jack Russell. The playful Jack Russell is a smart and loyal pet.

A Hunter's Helper

At one time, all dogs had unique purposes. The Jack Russell's purpose was to help hunters. Hunters used them to chase animals that ran into underground tunnels. The Jack Russell terrier was perfect for this job because of its small size and fearless attitude. These characteristics are still found in today's Jack Russells.

Jack Russell terriers are active dogs. They enjoy agility courses.

Jack Russells have a strong hunting **instinct**. Instincts can be developed, but they can't be taught. Today, a few hunters still use Jack Russells.

Most Jack Russell terriers, however, are kept as pets. It's important for owners to understand the natural instincts of the breed. Jack Russells will chase just about anything. They'll sprint after squirrels or rabbits outdoors. Indoors, they'll chase smaller pets. A Jack Russell can hurt a small animal if it catches it.

instinct — a behavior an animal knows at birth and does not have to learn

Puppies from responsible breeders are healthy and have fun personalities.

People who want a Jack Russell should learn as much as they can about the breed. Potential owners should decide whether they have the time and patience to deal with this active and smart breed. They should get their puppy from a responsible **breeder**. Good breeders make sure their dogs are healthy and have the best breed qualities.

breeder — someone who breeds and raises dogs

People who want a Jack Russell also should be sure they get the kind of terrier they expect. Over the years, there has been much confusion about the Jack Russell terrier breed.

The name Jack Russell terrier is used to describe a group of small terriers that all have a similar look. These dogs have white coats and black or tan markings. The difference between the terriers lies in their height.

The terrier recognized by the American Kennel Club (AKC) is called the Parson Russell terrier. But many people refer to these dogs as Jack Russells. People who breed Parson Russell terriers for AKC shows must follow a **breed standard**. Their terriers must stand 12 to 14 inches (30 to 36 centimeters) tall. Other dogs called Jack Russells can be 10 to 15 inches (25 to 38 centimeters) tall. These dogs cannot compete in AKC events.

breed standard — the physical features of a breed that judges look for in a dog show

Dog show judges study each dog to make sure it meets the breed standard.

EDGE FACT

The American Kennel Club accepted the Jack Russell terrier breed in 2000. In 2003, the name was changed to the Parson Russell terrier.

CHAPTER 2

THE PARSON'S DOGS

The Jack Russell terrier was named after **Parson** John Russell. He lived in England in the early 1800s. Called "Jack" by his friends, Parson Russell enjoyed foxhunting. He bred dogs that helped him hunt.

In 1819, Russell bought a fox terrier from a milkman. The dog's name was Trump. She was about the size of a female fox. When Russell bred Trump with his own foxhunting dogs, a new type of terrier was born. These puppies were the very first Jack Russell terriers.

parson — **a religious leader of a church**

Parson John Russell bred the first Jack Russell terriers.

Jack Russell terriers are focused and determined hunting dogs.

Early Jack Russell terriers showed a great talent for hunting. They found and **flushed** game quickly, without killing the animal. Parson Russell and other hunters liked that these dogs did not attack prey. They believed a dog that killed prey gave a hunter an unfair advantage. Many hunters today also value this skill. Like their ancestors, today's Jack Russell terriers are brave and fast. They seem to truly understand their place as the hunter's helper.

EDGE FACT

Parson Russell's terriers were white. They had tan or black markings on their heads and at the base of their tails.

flush — to drive an animal out from its hiding place

CHAPTER 3

SMALL BUT STRONG

Jack Russell terriers are mostly white with black or tan markings. A Jack Russell terrier with both black and tan marks is called tricolored. Grizzle is another color pattern for this breed. All the hairs on a grizzle dog are tipped with a darker color.

A Jack Russell terrier can have a smooth, rough, or broken coat. A dog with a smooth coat has short hair covering its body. A Jack Russell with a rough coat has longer hair. A broken coat falls in the middle, with longer hair only on certain parts of the body. All three coat types are coarse, not soft. Coarse coats help keep dogs dry and warm in cold, wet weather.

Puppies from the same mother can have different types of coats.

A Born Athlete

The Jack Russell terrier is small but athletic. The dog's entire body is strong. Its back legs are especially muscular. They allow Jack Russells to move quickly. The Jack Russell has a narrow chest and shoulders. These features allow it to crawl into tunnels to chase after foxes and other animals.

The Jack Russell's ears complete its look. They are small and fall forward from the top. People sometimes call them drop ears.

Unless owners train them not to, Jack Russell terriers will dig uncontrollably.

Jack Russell terriers are small but speedy.

Temperament

If left alone all day, a Jack Russell will find plenty of trouble. These smart little dogs can cause a lot of damage when they're bored. They might chew on furniture or clothing. They can get into garbage or destroy curtains and window blinds. Some owners joke that Jack Russell terriers think shoes are a food group.

Jack Russell terriers enjoy playing fetch and other games.

EDGE FACT

A Jack Russell terrier should be kept on a leash in public places. Even a well-trained Jack Russell terrier will follow its hunting instincts before its owner's commands.

Owners who leave their Jack Russell alone for long
periods of time must help their dog stay busy. Some
owners leave out plenty of dog toys for their Jack
[text obscured] their dogs rawhide bones

[text obscured] the high-energy Jack
[text obscured] fore leaving it alone.
[text obscured] loors will help tire out

[text obscured] re bred to hunt alone,
[text obscured] nly dog in a home.
[text obscured] Jack Russell and another
[text obscured] gether peacefully.
[text obscured] ive with smaller pets
[text obscured] e breed's instinct to chase
[text obscured] er any training.
[text obscured] the best pets for families
[text obscured] rriers can get along with
[text obscured] But very young children
[text obscured] mall animals. They may
[text obscured] Even the gentlest
Jack Russell may bite a child who treats it roughly.

CHAPTER 4

CARING FOR A JACK RUSSELL

Some people think that smaller dogs need less care than larger ones. But that isn't true. Owning a dog of any size is a big responsibility.

Training

Jack Russell terriers are stubborn. Owners must begin training their puppies as soon as they bring them home. A Jack Russell terrier puppy should be taught to walk on a leash. It should also be trained to come when it is called. Other important commands include "sit," "down," and "drop it." The best way to get a Jack Russell terrier to repeat a desired behavior is with rewards. Jack Russell terriers respond best to lots of attention and treats.

Jack Russells are very loyal to their owners.

Unfortunately, many Jack Russell terriers delight in doing things that most owners don't like. Most of these behaviors are a result of the dog's natural instincts. They include barking, digging, and chasing small animals. For this reason, it's important to begin training early. It's much easier to teach good behaviors than it is to undo bad ones.

Plenty of exercise for the active Jack Russell will help discourage behavior problems. A tired dog doesn't have as much energy to get into trouble.

Because of their hunting instincts, Jack Russell terriers enjoy chasing balls.

A low-protein food may help calm a hyper Jack Russell terrier.

Feeding

Jack Russell terriers eat far less food than larger dogs. They need healthy food. Dog food sold at pet supply stores is usually healthier than food found at grocery stores. It may also be more expensive.

By-products are parts of an animal that are unfit for people to eat. But they are often used by pet food companies. Dog food without by-products is heathier for your Jack Russell.

Preservatives in dog food help keep it fresh. But chemical preservatives should be avoided. Tocopherols are natural preservatives made from vitamins. The food for your Jack Russell should be preserved with tocopherols.

Some dog owners cook fresh food for their pets. Dogs can eat most fruits, vegetables, and lean meats. But you should never give your Jack Russell onions or chocolate. These foods are **toxic** to dogs. Just a small amount of chocolate could be deadly to your small dog.

Grooming

A Jack Russell's short coat doesn't need a lot of grooming. Brushing a Jack Russell's coat at least once a week keeps it clean and free of dead hair. Some owners use a special brush to strip their dog's coat of longer hair. A stripping brush leaves the dog with a smoother-looking coat than a regular brush does.

Other important jobs include cleaning the dog's ears, trimming its toenails, and brushing its teeth. Clean ears usually don't get infected. Short toenails won't snag carpets or clothing. Keeping a dog's teeth clean helps the dog stay healthy. Remember to use products made for dogs when cleaning their ears and brushing their teeth. Human products can make dogs sick.

A Jack Russell with a rough coat must be groomed more often than one with a smooth coat.

Keeping a Jack Russell Terrier Healthy

Like all dogs, Jack Russells should regularly visit a veterinarian, or vet. A vet is a doctor who treats animals. Puppies need to receive **vaccinations** from a vet. Adult dogs need yearly vet visits. A vet will weigh your dog, take its temperature, and look for signs of sickness.

Taking care of your Jack Russell's health is part of being a responsible pet owner. Having your dog spayed or neutered is another part. These operations prevent the dogs from producing offspring. This helps lower the number of unwanted pets in the world. The operations also reduce the dogs' risk for cancer.

Keeping a Jack Russell terrier happy and healthy is a big job. But it's a job with many rewards if the breed is right for you. You could hunt high and low and never find a better pet than the Jack Russell terrier.

vaccination — medicine that protects animals from disease

A Jack Russell terrier is a very rewarding pet for the right owner.

Glossary

breed (BREED) — a certain kind of animal within an animal group; breed also means to mate and raise a certain kind of dog.

breeder (BREE-duhr) — someone who breeds and raises dogs or other animals

breed standard (BREED STAN-durd) — the physical features of a breed that judges look for in a dog show

flush (FLUSH) — to drive an animal out from its hiding place

instinct (IN-stingkt) — behavior that an animal knows at birth and does not have to learn

parson (PAR-son) — a religious leader of a church

toxic (TOK-sik) — poisonous

vaccination (vak-suh-NAY-shun) — a shot of medicine that protects animals from a disease

Read More

Morgan, Diane. *Parson and Jack Russell Terriers.* Animal Planet Pet Care Library. Neptune City, N.J.: T.F.H. Publications, 2007.

Murray, Julie. *Jack Russell Terriers.* Animal Kingdom. Edina, Minn.: Abdo, 2005.

Waters, Jo. *The Wild Side of Pet Dogs.* Raintree Perspectives. Chicago: Raintree, 2005.

Internet Sites

FactHound offers a safe, fun way to find educator-approved Internet sites related to this book.

Here's what you do:

1. Visit *www.facthound.com*
2. Choose your grade level.
3. Begin your search.

This book's ID number is 9781429623025.

FactHound will fetch the best sites for you!

Index